Metamorphosis

**A SERIES OF SHORT ESSAYS EXPLORING
LIFE'S QUESTIONS AND LESSONS**

TIVOLI SURESH CHHABRIYA

First paperback edition: November 2024

Design by Vanessa Mendozzi
Edited by Crystal Nero
Proofread by Trinity M.

ISBN Paperback - 979-8-9919197-5-3
ISBN Ebook - 979-8-9919197-4-6
ISBN Hardcover - 979-8-9919197-3-9

To my husband, kids, parents and sister—
thank you for being my rock through
everything in life.

CONTENTS

If you want to know
where to find your
contribution to the
world, look at your
wounds. When you
learn how to heal
them, teach others.

— Emily Maroutian

Why I Wrote this Book

Words matter.

What we say, to whom we say it, and how we say it matters. Irrespective of who we are and what we do for a living, what ties us all together is our humanness, our humanity, our sense of connectedness—and the way we connect with one another is through these words. Words are powerful and can change us in ways we can't even imagine, but only if we're willing to brave the journey by going down that road and allowing them to.

Whether we are CEOs, athletes, movie stars, frontline workers, doctors, or accountants, we all experience similar emotions and feelings in our lives - this is what makes us who we are and eventually forms a significant part of our core. When life gets complex, navigating the various emotions can make us feel very lonely. In the thick of it, we sometimes feel like we must be the only ones thinking or going through these things. When I was going through a difficult time in my own life and I read about other people's life stories, I suddenly felt calmer and more at peace. When I was exposed to other people's experiences and saw how raw and real things can get in their lives too, it all started making more sense in my own life.

That's the thing about words—they don't just make us

feel heard, they also make us feel seen and understood. We can make better sense of what we feel when we are able to communicate with one another. We are able to understand what we are going through better when we read about what others are going through or have gone through, as well as what they are feeling.

We feel less alone then, less misunderstood.

We are all thrown curveballs at different times in our lives, but the question always remains: *What will we end up doing with those curveballs?* Do we just let them get us down and stay there, or do we learn to find the courage to pick ourselves back up so we can live the best lives we possibly can?

We don't always have answers, and I have learned over time that that's okay. Answers can be overrated, because a lot of our healing takes place through the tough questions we are willing to ask in life. Sometimes asking the right questions is in itself enough to get our minds thinking about the things that truly matter in life. It was through my own journey of trying to make sense of my life that I discovered the power of words and how they were able to change my life.

This book is an ode to my love for words and my sincerest expression of gratitude to these words for helping me find more meaning in my own existence, in ways I could not have imagined possible, and in times I needed them the most. My hope is that this book gives you some of the words that you've also been looking for in life, to not just feel heard, but also seen—for who you've been, who you are, and who you are becoming.

The picture will not always be perfect, but how will we grow if we don't have anything to grow from?

Guide to This Book

If you are wondering where to start, try taking a look inside yourself. What are you feeling today? Begin with an honest understanding of your emotions first. Think about what your mind is saying. Do you feel overwhelmed, sad, excited, joyful? Once you recognize your thoughts in the present moment, look at the contents and pick a topic based on what speaks to you. This book is divided into two sections that are designed to meet you where you are. *Pause, so you can reflect*, and *Move, when you are ready for change.*

Pause: So You Can Reflect

Part One is for when you've known for a long time that you need to slow down but haven't either found the time or the reason to. This section urges you to take some time out of your busy life to lay in your thoughts. To be able to just listen to your mind and your heart; hear what they are saying and give yourself a chance to look at these emotions objectively and honestly.

Reflect is for when you're ready for deeper introspection—of life and of your emotions. Reflect not only allows you to think about your life in a way you possibly may not have done before, but also in the process gives you ideas to be able to navigate some of the complexities of life. It gives you permission to take up some much-needed space in your life so you can grow into the person you are meant to be. This section is intertwined with Pause, so you can see the overlap and overlay of emotions and thoughts as you go in and out.

Move: When You Are Ready for Change

Part Two is for when you have paused and reflected for a while, and things somewhat make more sense now. You have looked inward and worked on yourself and feel like you understand the myriad of emotions a bit more—you are ready to move forward in your healing journey, and you're looking for more ways to do that.

Read this book at your own pace, whether it's one chapter at a time or one paragraph at a time. Let the thoughts and emotions you feel soak in. Some chapters are heavier than others, so don't feel the need to rush. Let it move you, sit with you, shape you. Let it remain inside you and see where it can take you.

PART ONE

PAUSE, So You Can Reflect

1.

DISCONNECT(ED)

If you are feeling disconnected—either from the world, or from yourself—read this to make more sense of that feeling and to find your connection again.

Dis.con.nect - break the connection of or between.

It's ironic that, as humans, the thing that we are built for the most is connection—but in today's modern, uber-connected world, it's probably this very thing that brings us down or drains us the most. We now know what's happening in each other's lives at the touch of a few buttons, and we sometimes feel the need to share the smallest details of our own lives—what we cook, eat, where we go, who we meet, and when we work out. In the midst of all this, do we ever stop to wonder if what we think of as connection in terms of sharing, we lose in being present and sometimes even in being real?

We seem satisfied with the many likes of strangers we haven't met, yet nothing can replace the warmth of a few loved ones. We're in this cycle of showing the good lives we live, but some of us have lost touch with what makes it truly great. We are more connected than ever, yet we feel lonelier. How are more and more of us feeling disconnected during such overly connected times? What are we doing wrong? It feels like the connection within us is broken, and sometimes the connection between ourselves feels distant too. We might physically be in one place, but our minds are occupied—not just with thoughts of our lives, but with details of others' lives too. Even when we are with our loved ones, are we really as present today as we used to be? As present as we can be?

We can travel to most parts of the world, buy anything

with three clicks and get it almost instantly delivered to our doorstep, communicate with our loved ones living in different parts of the world more easily than ever; yet we feel a void inside that's becoming harder to fill with what we see and do online. We reminisce about the old, simpler times, but find it hard to weave a way out of the busy lives we keep building for ourselves. It's a vicious circle we have found ourselves in. I often wonder, are these conscious choices ones we really want, or choices that we simply make because of what we see around us?

Even though we can have instant communication, we seem to have fallen behind in long-term, deep connection. We share small details of our lives with the world, but we keep the biggest truths hidden from ourselves. It's so much easier to talk about what's on the surface than it is to dig deep in, but who are we really fooling in the bargain? There are times we become obsessed with this idea of sharing all our good moments, while believing that no one has a dull day in their life; but we forget that it is in the difficult moments that we know who we really are and what we're made of. It is in the moments when we cry that we realize we are not really as okay as we thought we were. In the moments that we feel regret, we also realize that we need to make a change to our current circumstances. In the moments that we feel fear, we also learn to find the courage to move ahead. In our moments of doubt also lies the revelation of what we are really capable of as individuals. Yet, we do not believe that these are the moments that truly change our lives for the better, simply because the online world has shown us their highlight reel. These feelings are not wrong, and our lives are not bad if we don't have the perfect squares of perfectly curated times. Craving the perfect-looking boxes of someone else's life would be a complete waste of what our own journey has to offer. We are imperfect, but it is in these imperfections that our growth really happens, and all the life lessons that go with it. Without them, our lives will look perfect on the outside, yet can feel empty on the inside. Our lives are real, meant to be lived, and so are we. Then why have we deluded ourselves into thinking that the world of make-believe that we see online is the real deal? We see so little of a person's journey, yet we believe so much. What we see are snippets of people's lives, forgetting that there is another reality behind the scenes. Have we really become so shallow?

Our worlds are colliding and merging today in an attempt to show how good our lives are, but all we need to do to live a good life is pave the way for ourselves and build one based on how everything feels. We seem satisfied if our lives look good on the outside, even though it hurts on the inside, because sometimes it's easier to pretend than to feel.

But at this rate of constant sharing and comparing, at what point will we feel like our lives are enough? That we are enough? How do we measure the end point for all this over the course of our lives?

Is it when we show the world that we have a better car than they do (than who?), or is it when we share our luxurious holiday online for everyone to see? What if working hard to own the car of our dreams—whatever that might be— is what makes us feel good? Or what if soaking in the moment, being present, and really unwinding with our loved ones is what we need? Some of us have become content showing that we are traveling the world, even though we feel loneliness inside—continuously accompanied by strangers, but craving our own company within. Are we scared to connect to ourselves when we can so easily communicate with the world, because we are afraid of what we might find and who we might become? Or more importantly, are we afraid of becoming the best version of ourselves so we won't have anything to complain about anymore?

In a world where we have accepted dishonesty to the point of losing real connections, how long are we all willing to play this game, and at what cost? For some of us, there comes a time when we decide the game stops the moment we stop playing it. We know we've done it long enough and have been losing ourselves bit by bit, realizing that's not the direction we want for our lives. We stop dancing to the tunes of others' lives, we stop traveling to the destinations of other people's choices, we stop choosing careers based on other people's lifestyles. It is then that we find that we can actually live a life in tune with what we love, what satisfies us and what truly connects us to ourselves. Our lives will not be perfect, and it will certainly not be fun at all times, and most of the pieces of our journey might not make it to the squares—but it will be honest, real, and ours.

There will come a time when we understand that the best way to connect to ourselves is in fact by disconnecting from the world around for a bit—delete that app, say no to invitations that drain you, choose to stay in and read on a Friday night, take that vacation you have been planning, be present in the moment with loved ones, and choose what you want over what the world does. Not everyone needs to be aware of the details of your days. Not everyone needs to know all the ups and downs in your life; maybe there are some parts that are best reserved for us and our loved ones. Maybe we can learn to build just a little circle around us, one that actually helps us retain our connection to our core. We can learn to protect this circle and ourselves within it. We can learn to shield ourselves from the opinions of others and let the love of those who matter seep through. We can learn to finally quiet the noise of the outside world and listen to the voices of those who truly matter. We can allow ourselves to slow down our pace, even if for a bit, and learn to just breathe.

So maybe being disconnected is not a bad thing after all.

2.

PAUSE

If you've constantly been on the go, just to be able to get by—read this to understand what may be going on in your mind and your heart. You can then create some space between what's happening in the moment, and how you respond to it.

Life takes us through many detours, some planned and some unplanned. Different detours put us in different modes in our lives—in some, we may see ourselves grow. In others, we might see ourselves break.

When we are experiencing big, life-changing events, like the loss of a loved one, we know the profound impact it's having on us. The event not only impacts our lives externally, but unconsciously—we may let a part of ourselves die too. We lose moments and are instead left with memories, we lose love and are left with grief, we lose hope and are left with a void—a void that may never be filled up. And we let that event move us in such a way that it ultimately shifts who we are, changes life for us as we know it, changes us as we knew we were.

Then there are those micro-shifts that happen within us where we see pieces of ourselves break away. Those are harder to recognize, as they are very subtle. For example, when we see an unfulfilled dream slip away, it sometimes turns into many unfulfilled dreams. When we feel more hopelessness than hope, we see more obstacles than pathways leading us to the light at the end of the road, leading us to the light within; and we somehow convince ourselves that this is life. This is how it is for many of us, and this is probably how it's meant to be for us too. We see these micro-shifts chipping away at our core, more and more as our new reality – the new norm for us. It happens so gradually over time that even the awareness doesn't really need us to change in any big way. This is why it can be so misleading—our reality shifts right from underneath us without us realizing it. The mistake we make is in the very acceptance of these micro-shifts as our new reality.

Many of us were never really taught how to deal with tough life changes, even the big ones, let alone the "minor" discomforts we tend to feel. That uncomfortable feeling in your gut, that unease when you are around someone or while you are watching something wrong take place. We didn't always have emotionally intelligent conversations about the hard truths life throws at us; and the smaller ones that we consider less impactful actually run very deep into the fabric of our being. Our immediate response to these little feelings has usually been to ignore them, so we were never really taught how to unpack what they were trying to tell us. They're not large enough to demand our immediate attention, so we tend to push them back—to the back of our minds and the back of our lives. Not having the language or consciousness of talking about these smaller discomforts then turns into an uncomfortable acceptance of current reality for us and before we know it, we can't seem to recognize ourselves or our lives anymore.

So how do we start understanding the layers behind these discomforts? Every time we take stock of how we feel, they're still there—they creep up every single day and don't really go away. What do we do with them, how do we treat them? Where do we start? Or do we even start? What if we're opening up Pandora's box as we start asking these questions? We may wonder if we will find more than we can handle in our current circumstances. We check our calendars, make mental notes of what all we have on our to-do lists – do we really have the bandwidth to deal with it right now?

But if not now, then when?

When we look back at the series of events that led to these current truths we are faced with, we realize that we might have been in survival mode all along. Life didn't feel good, but we still moved. It wasn't fulfilling, but we still went on. We had things to do, places to be, people to take care of. What was once a life we had envisioned with many big dreams, has turned into an adjusted version of reality, mostly projected by others' expectations and limitations set for us. We tell ourselves that the dreams felt too big for us and the adjusted reality seems more realistic. But who are we really to decide what's big and what can be real? Is it not just an illusion we have created in our own minds based on what society shows us and our own perceptions of it? What we have seen in the past and think we continue to see? But our perceptions can be misleading sometimes. When we're experiencing what feels like a breakdown, maybe it is really the shedding of pieces we know we no longer need, so that what remains can come together to become our true self. What if we're viewing something as holding us back, when it is actually catapulting us forward into a life that we only dreamed of but never imagined as a reality? Our views can get so skewed based on what has worked in the past, or seemed to have worked until now, that we become unwilling to look beyond what has been to understand all that can be.

We saw the shifts happening around us—the changes, the growth, the movements—and wondered why nothing moved for us the way we thought it would. These questions were easy to ask—the tough part was coming up with the answers. We saw people travel, move to different cities, quit their jobs and start new ones, break up with toxic relationships to find more peaceful ones. But when we looked at our lives, nothing significantly changed for us in ways that we would have liked. Life kept going and people changed, but we remained the same. Things moved forward, but we were stagnant. It's almost as if we were too scared to change and that led us to remaining stuck, only to one day wake up and realize that this is not the life we thought we'd be living.

Unfortunately, there is no quick and easy way to get from this point to the other side of living a life we have always imagined. We have to go through the process of being honest with ourselves about what we truly want from our lives and sitting in our uncomfortable feelings for a bit. We have to listen to our own voices, to our hearts beating one beat at a time. We will go through many ups and downs through this process, many doubts, questions and fears will arise, making us question it all - ourselves, our lives, our choices along the way, and even this process. But the more we stick with it, the more we might start feeling at peace.

It may not be a sudden shift, but one day we will realize that we're more at peace today than we were yesterday. And the day before. We will stop having as many questions, or the questions won't seem to have the same impact it did on us before. Through the process of us dealing with our pain and understanding the root causes of our feelings, we will start to believe that things will be okay, and we can in fact live a life filled with all that we want. We will have a stronger sense of where we have reached, understanding that it took many different paths and choices for us to get to where we are. And it's no coincidence that it all worked out this way. There was intentionality from our side, with a sprinkle of magic from the universe to make sure that our roads converged into the life we are living. And then slowly these micro-shifts in peace add up to a lingering joy; or at least the beginnings of it. We start seeing rays of hope, building on each other to show us a giant pathway filled with light. What was unfamiliar once, starts feeling more and more familiar. The calm and peace spreads over our lives. We feel alive again.

The dreams start to surface once more—not all of them at once, but traces of them, a sprinkling here and there. If we don't pay close attention to these micro-shifts of change happening within us, there's a good chance we will let life pass us by. But if we do, we know that there's still time. There's still time to make our dreams come true, there's still time to find joy again, there's still time to be hopeful. Not all is lost.

What felt like the end of the road was truly a bend. Life may have taken you through many unplanned detours, but your dreams remained yours and met you on the other side of what could have been.

3.

OUR EVOLVED SELVES LOOKING AT OUR PAST SELVES

*If you've felt like you don't quite belong, read
this to help you understand yourself a bit
better and to feel a little less alone.*

So often, women are raised to be simple. The good girls next door. We are taught to be less complex and more accommodating. *Questioning* in general may not have been encouraged. Some of us are taught that life could be tougher for us if we are complicated; and that's not a good thing.

I often questioned things in life growing up—it seemed like I had more questions than I should be asking and found fewer answers than I would have liked. I didn't quite understand why others were so easily able to accept things the way they were and why some things in life seemed the way they did. I thought that being different was bad because you don't quite fit in with the majority of those around you. By the very definition, different meant *not the same as others.* You don't fit into any of the regular molds, and you certainly don't fit into the box society has made for its women. And if you're not outrageously different, you don't quite fit into that *rebellious* box either. *But where do I really fit in?* I often wondered. I believed in making my own choices—some were defiant, some were compliant. I didn't want anyone's formula to life and wanted to write my own equations to figure out what worked for me.

For a long time (a long, long time), things just didn't add up. When you are looking for your own equation in life, you often feel alone. I wondered what life would look like if I were "simple" like I was told. How much easier would life be then? I thought of the women who went about life as expected, within the lines. I wondered why I wasn't like that. I wasn't an overtly complicated or defiant person; I was outwardly kind and compliant, but inwardly unhappy. I was searching for myself and for answers to all the questions about life I had. I often wondered if others questioned as much as I did. Or was it just me? I tried to trace my path, looking over at my journey through a magnifying glass so I could find some event, some situation, some interaction that explained why I was *just different*.

When I looked at life's choices, I didn't see what many others saw. I didn't see the conventional, get a job, marry the "right" person, have kids, and retire path for myself. Life just *did not* equal that for me. I didn't know what it equaled, but I knew that it certainly had to have more layers and emotions. Like, where was love, and regret, and passion, and anger, and frustration, and disappointment in all of this? Hadn't all of that shaped us into the people we are today, who know better than to simply make choices with our heads instead of our hearts? Were we really so out of touch with ourselves, or were we just eager to please those around us? In our quest to be simple, uncomplicated people, we had lost the essence of who we really were deep down. Because going down deep to understand yourself is complicated work in itself.

We were so busy trying to be the right thing for the people around us, that we forgot what the best thing for ourselves was. We accepted things in life as they came—simple and uncomplicated. That's because somewhere along the way we started equating different to bad. But as I observed those around me making different choices and being different people, I realized that different was not bad.

**Different was actually bold, and honest,
and courageous, and beautiful, and strong,
and lovely, and free, and liberated.**

Different means that you don't need to fit into any specific criteria, check any specific boxes like the others did—you can create your very own boxes to check off in life. We can sometimes be a blank piece of paper, and other times have color all over. I was different, and hence could create my own definition for what I wanted to be, who I wanted to be, and when I wanted to be. In essence, being free of limitations resulted in a freedom from expectations.

Sometimes different may look good, and sometimes messy. Different is a path that hasn't been defined—it is the unknown. Different may mean out of bounds, drawing outside the lines. Different may also mean crazy and beautiful, chaos and order, scary and joyous, all at the same time.

Whoever told you different was bad had not really lived, or loved.

Different means that you are strong enough and beautiful enough to dig deep to understand what makes life for you— what makes this complicated mess such a beautiful piece of art, such a magnificent thing, at the end of it all. You do not have to be concerned with the life paths others take and choose, because you have built enough resilience to build one for yourself, no matter how it looks. If life weren't messy and you weren't courageous enough to create a mess, you simply have not been living at all. It means you've just been using a manual handed over to you and have followed all the instructions to ensure that every step was correctly followed right after the one before. You've been living life so close to the center and scared to walk on the edges, for what if you fall and create a mess.

But darling, if you don't ever try, how will you ever know?

If you don't ever let yourself fall, how will you learn to pick yourself back up again? If you don't ever love, how will you feel heartbreak? If you don't ever let yourself feel sad, how will you know happiness? If you don't ever make bad choices, how will you know the good ones when it's time to make them?

If you are too afraid to live at all, what will you call "life" at the end of it all?

4.

THE FORMULA TO LIFE

*If you believed in a formula to life growing up
but realize as an adult that the math doesn't
quite add up.*

Have you ever found yourself wondering if there was a formula to life that someone could just hand over to you to follow? Wouldn't everything be much simpler and easier then? As we adult, and are faced with many choices and challenges in life, it sometimes feels easier knowing what our next step should be. From the small choices to the big ones, we find ourselves spending much of our time each day figuring out which path is the best one for us. I know for sure there have been moments I wished for a genie to come hand me a formula, but I also very quickly realized that no genie was coming along, and life was left for us to figure out as we move forward. One thing I have come to understand with certainty is that what applies to one individual does not necessarily apply to another, and what made sense for us growing up need not be the case now.

Growing up, I believed that there was a formula to life. I strongly focused on good grades in school, knowing for sure that it would ultimately lead to success in life. It's what we've been told and taught repeatedly—almost as if someone had cracked the equation to life and handed it over to us to follow through if we wanted the same end result as them. This is not bad or wrong; it's just that we need to think about if that's what is meant for us and if the math adds up to what we're looking for in life. Good grades in school do not necessarily translate to success in life, and the very definition of success has evolved over time.

Even though I was a straight-A student in school, I was not able to get away from the tough choices life had in store for me. I found myself in situations where I had to make a choice between kindness toward others or kindness toward myself; between doing what's best for my life or for my loved ones' happiness; following a path true to my calling or satisfying others' ambitions. Making one choice felt like a success to me, while it looked like a failure to others. I often wondered how this happened to me. I was stumped. I didn't know which rule book I could quickly pull out to reference the right answer in these situations. I didn't know which guide I should be using. I thought I did everything right in life. I was a textbook child—worked hard, was a good student, an obedient child, no trouble at all. So how did I find myself in situations I would not have been able to fathom? How did my good grades in school not translate to obvious success in life like I had been told?

What did I do wrong?

This made me think about the quintessential definition of success we've been given. Back in the day, more money, better cars, and large homes were the definition of success and happiness. Somewhere within, I knew that I had to question the definition that was handed to us on a platter. I wondered if this idea of success and the concept of happiness could change. Wasn't there more to life and its essence? What were we missing by being so focused on *just one* area? You see more and more people today choosing careers that make them feel fulfilled, sometimes even at the cost of making less money. You see more people leaving marriages that they are unhappy in because they value their happiness more than what society would perceive of it, or them. This is not just a trend that people are following, but a pattern that shows us that more people are finally following their hearts today over what their minds have been trained to do.

Even so, we still see some struggling with this. Why is it that some of them have cracked the formula to what truly matters in life, while others are still struggling? Happiness in one area of life has come at the cost of another, and many people find themselves a little dissatisfied. How did this happen? Did we just let society dictate what's important for so long that we actually forgot to think for ourselves? Have we been thinking more about where we're at in the rat race and our paychecks, that we lost sight of true relationships, patience, and love in the bargain? *Or did we just have ourselves wired wrong all along?*

Many of us may wake up decades later to realize that we've actually been living life backwards. By focusing on what looked good, we didn't pay enough attention to how that made us feel. We could wake up one day to realize that the formula we were given didn't quite equate to our own definition of success and happiness in life. The math just didn't add up for us. There are so many areas this way of thinking has left an impact on – our friendships, family, finances, career. This way of thinking has touched every area. We may have lost true friends along the way as we built our career and finances, or we lost touch with family who didn't grow at the pace we did. But when we do find ourselves in such a position as we get older, how do we work to rewire our brains and unlearn all that we've been taught? Have we really stopped to think if the life we are living is what we really want, or are we just too scared to question because we don't know what we'll do with the answers we find?

Where do we even start?

We start by thinking about what we really want our lives to be defined by, the quality or quantity of all the things and people we surround ourselves with. Do we still want to hold on to the belief that success means high-paying jobs—even if these make us feel empty at our core? Or do we finally want to be honest with ourselves about what makes us come alive and give ourselves a real shot at finding meaning in our work? Do we still want to continue using the same formula we were taught, or do we want to understand where we're at in life now and realign ourselves to what matters to us today? When I see that some people who could not crack the math equations in school have actually found the secret to a happy life, I wonder - what did they do differently, that others got wrong?

Were they just more in alignment with what their hearts wanted? Did they have the courage to dance to their own tunes, even though there was different music playing? Did they choose love over and over again? When I see some people truly thriving in life and loving what they do, I often think that, along with making different choices, they seem to just have a different mindset altogether. Maybe they were given different manuals to follow and were taught different things. Maybe they valued different virtues over others. Did they pay more attention to their hearts, because they knew their minds were just not into it? Did they learn to build courage and resilience that got them through difficult times, so they didn't find themselves shattered when the first thing didn't go right? Did they learn how to make friends more easily and be happy with the little things in life, instead of waiting for the big milestones?

I believe that some of them definitely built better emotional or relationship intelligence—not just cognitive intelligence—which contributed to them making different choices in life. They also understand that the formula to life is that *there is none*.

I wonder, if we all started living life the way we have always wanted, would we feel like we can be truly happy? Would we feel like the chase has finally stopped and that we could start just being and living?

5.

LIFE AND ITS MANY CONTRADICTIONS

Life can be full of contradictions. As we grow, we find more of these in our lives, and we learn that these contradictions can all actually coexist.

As we adult through life and its many challenges, becoming the people we were meant to be and living the lives we were meant to live, we will catch ourselves by surprise many times. There's a funny thing that happens as we get older—some of us tend to go back to our roots more. The very roots we questioned growing up.

In our youth we may have thought they they we were a bit too deep and old for us. A bit outdated, like they did not belong in our lives or were not relevant to us. As we grow, though, we come to understand the strength of these roots that have provided for us for generations. They are the very reason for us being able to stand as strong as we do. Because of the strength of these roots below us, we can go deep within ourselves, knowing that our foundations are solid.

This is something we sometimes take for granted.

As we evolve and move forward in our lives, we also tend to go back to the places we may have wanted to get away from, places we could not identify with or felt we couldn't grow in. They remind us of who we used to be before all these big dreams, goals, and milestones came along. When life was enough as is, and we were enough as we were. Things were simple, uncomplicated - allowing us to be who we wanted to be, when we wanted to be. There were no checklists and bucket lists that our lives were defined by. We let ourselves define each moment as it came, because we didn't think we had anything to prove to anyone. No societal expectations and projections dominating our sense of worth, and our sense of what life should look like. We also tend to go back to these places because it felt lighter, easier—like you just knew things would work out, fall into place. You had no reason to believe otherwise. Nothing or no one told you that there was a chance life may be harder than you think, that you might have tougher battles to face than you are prepared for, greater obstacles to overcome than you were previously faced with.

We lived life with our starry eyes and ruthless determination to get what we wanted to in life. And even if people told us about the potential negatives, we wouldn't want to believe them anyway. We had youth on our side; optimism and hopefulness were the virtues that drove us strongly toward our dreams and our goals. But as we "adult" and face life on our own, we realize that life can be a bit tougher than we think, and full of contradictions we never thought were possible.

You can keep going and can feel stuck. You are afraid, yet learn to build courage. Hope and hopelessness almost coexist daily. You feel modern yet keep going back to your roots. You question life and its many contractions because you were almost expecting to deal with just one of these but realize more and more that they can all coexist and *will* coexist, whether we are prepared for them or not. In the grand scheme of things, a lot of what life offers us is not mutually exclusive. As we learn to let go of sadness, we feel happiness. As we learn to let go of our negativity, we feel more optimistic. As we build more strength, we let go of our weaknesses. These all come in and out of our lives, overlapping each other so beautifully and fully, that we can't feel *whole* without all of them. We somehow can't understand one without the other; the role each of these emotions plays in our lives is independently and cohesively necessary to our existence.

If we once thought that we needed only one or the other emotion in life, not only to exist but to thrive, we realize we don't need just one of these to become who we were meant to be and to live a full life. *We need them all.*

6.

HOME

If you've always wondered where home is or what home is, read this to see if any of the following definitions of home resonate with you.

Home, the most beautiful place we can be at. Home can mean different things to different people. For some it may be a physical structure, but for others it could be the people in those structures. But home does not necessarily have to either be a place or the people; it can also just be a feeling. Think about all the times when a person, place, or activity made you "feel at home." What exactly does that mean? Someone or something that instantly made us feel calm, at ease, like we belonged. Where it wasn't just ok that we were there, but that we were meant to be there. It was our place. Things just made more sense—we were more at peace with ourselves, not because the worries and sorrows had suddenly disappeared, but because we felt more in alignment with who we are. We may have found our strength to tackle life head-on in such places. We remembered who we have always been and were meant to be, before "life" happened and we let other people and circumstances dictate who we should be instead. We were more joyous in these places—something just clicked, something just fit. These places made us feel in sync with everything in our lives, because we knew that the direction we moved in from this place of home would be the right one.

If you've been looking for what *home* means to you, maybe you need to stop looking just for a place and start with understanding how you want to feel. Society has let us believe that our home is the place where we live, but I am here to tell you that your home is the place where you most feel like you belong. Home often is undefined, and different people get to define what home means to them. It really could just be a small speck or a vast feeling. It's truly not the size that matters, but the depth of emotions we are able to feel in that space. How much of ourselves we are willing to see and let be seen. A place where we feel like we were meant to be; a place we had been searching for but just hadn't found yet.

Whether it's a place or the people, whenever we do stumble upon such a home, suddenly the big deals in life don't seem as big anymore; the huge issues are not so huge anymore—they feel smaller, insignificant. In the vastness of the expanse you are in, in the depth of the feelings you feel, you are washed over by a slow wave of incredible peace, and everything else just seems to melt away. Everything else stops, everything else waits while you flow through this feeling of calmness, of gratitude, of amazingness. You breathe more slowly, like you are able to not just feel your breaths, but count them. You can feel the change that this deep breathing brings over you; you can feel the slow shifts happening inside you. You're sometimes not sure it exists, but it feels real. You don't know what it is, but you know it's there. Something so little, yet so moving. For a brief moment we can actually hear our own voices, our own minds, and feel what we are thinking.

So often we get lost in the idea of what we have believed this place could be—not realizing that it does not always have to be some extraordinary place that's hard to get to.

It could be as simple as a place down the road, the beach you've always gone to. What you need to do is listen to yourself to understand how you feel when you are in this place, and not what you think this place should look like. In the quiet moments when no one is listening, what is our heart trying to tell us? Where does our heart really want to be? What is it saying to us that we are sometimes not willing, or not wanting to listen to?

Finding such places is a matter of listening to our hearts.

Some may find that home for them is indeed a physical structure, but for others this place could mean constantly being on the move. Some may find their home in the mountains, while others may find it in the ocean. For some, their home can also be a person. A person who makes them feel seen, heard, and like they really belong; like they've known them forever, even though they haven't. Who understands them without the help of too many words, who finishes their sentences, who just *gets* it. Maybe a friend you have just met, but it feels like they have known your whole life story, someone you love talking to for hours. Some may find their home in books that just speak to them. Where they feel like the words were meant just for them, wondering how someone could literally be in their minds. Home could also mean a place in time for some. A memory that brings about a certain feeling. A time that you most loved and felt like you belonged.

You search for it as you get older, look for the familiar feelings, look for the familiar faces. Look to understand what's missing today that you once had. How you lost it and how you can find it again. Just a little bit more of that feeling, just a little more of feeling that alive again. That whole again, that full again. Like there's nothing missing, nothing's not the way it's not supposed to be. Nothing is off. Nothing has really shifted in the large scheme of things.

What we're really looking for in a home is what make us feel alive—where we can just feel all our emotions without judgment, without the heaviness, without the expectations. Just being in the moment. When we find such places later in life, we want to hold onto them tighter. Wanting to relive those moments again to feel alive some more. Wanting to *just be* a bit longer. Listen to our own voices more, listen to our hearts more. Feel the pause some more, feel the calmness a little bit longer.

No matter where we come from and what life we've lived, it's never too late to find our home.

7.

IN OUR ABILITY
TO FEEL, LIES OUR
POWER TO HEAL

If you've been feeling the pain for a long time,
but don't quite know how to process it.

Life is a journey. So many dreams, so many expectations, and so many hopes. It can be so beautiful, yet it is this very life that can also completely throw us off track. Expectations and reality will not always align, and when that happens it can leave us feeling a lot of pain.

We may feel disappointment in missed chances and opportunities, in people we once trusted, leaving us feeling lost and seeking validation. None of these things are easy to handle; they are hard emotions to cope with individually, and it can be even harder when they are combined together. Many times, we are in so much pain that we don't even recognize it, let alone process it. We are sometimes more concerned with showing that we are okay, because we don't even know where to start understanding how we really feel. Sometimes we are okay just being *okay,* because we don't know if we have the ability to deal with the pain. We are so caught up in just moving forward, that we put blinders on to do whatever needs to be done. This can lead us to living a life that we are superficially fine with, but deeply disconnected from and unhappy about. When people look at us and our lives, on the surface no one would even be able to know that we are unhappy. But every time there is a trigger in some form or the other, all the pain comes back up—in different forms and sizes and at unpredictable times. It can all sneak up so unexpectedly. When you see other people doing what you wish you'd done in life, when you go to places you wish you'd gone sooner, when you see others living life with courage each day, when you see people making brave decisions and choices that you wish you'd make.

Sometimes you think you are over the pain, or you've moved forward—and yet it keeps coming back up. It comes back up as a reminder that you still have healing to do, that you are not as okay as you think you are or as okay as you think *with who you are*. You still have work to do, looking inward and deep down and finding your truth.

Pain is also a reminder of the fact that you can actually feel happy. That you actually deserve happiness and the way you have been living with pain is not working anymore. That you are worthy of living with real happiness, and that pain and happiness don't always have to coexist in your life. You can have a life where these are mutually exclusive.

But when we are in so much pain, how do we let ourselves just feel happy? Where do we start the work even?

As contradictory as it may seem, the first step is letting yourself *feel the pain*. When we are willing to brave the depth of our emotions and feel, we can truly heal. When we let ourselves feel our pain, we are essentially acknowledging that we have been hurt, acknowledging that we deserve better, acknowledging that we can be more, and acknowledging that our life can be more. At the very basis of it, we are validating ourselves and our feelings; sometimes, that's all it takes to be able to start afresh. It can be hard because you don't know what you might find and what you'd do with what you find. It's scary—but healing as a process itself is scary, because at the very core of healing lies the idea that you are becoming a newer version of yourself. You are stepping out of your comfort zone to find a better way of being, a better you.

When you resist feeling the pain, you are also resisting becoming the best version of yourself, because there is no version of us *yet* without the pain. The pain is not just a teacher for where we might have gone wrong, but also how and where we can be better.

Resisting the pain is resisting living your life deeply—because if you go deep down, you will find the pain, and that hurts. But it's so important to let ourselves feel the pain—of shattered dreams, of lack of hope, of bitterness and what caused it, of what could have been versus what is. If we don't ever let ourselves feel the pain, we can be guaranteed to never be able to live a full life. Because in our pain also lies dreams and hopes that we may have let go of over time, but somehow, they still remain—unfinished and unfulfilled. In our pain, lies our healing. In our pain, lie glimpses of what could have been and what can be. In our pain, lies our courage, and in our pain, also lies our freedom and some of our answers.

Feeling your pain will lead to a lot of bitterness in the beginning. It will lead to a lot of anger, because the very fact that you are in pain means there's a part of you that feels you've been deeply wronged. You feel like a victim, you feel that life has been unfair. Whether or not that is objectively what happened is a different issue altogether. The point is that you are validating that part of you that feels like this.

When you acknowledge that you feel like a victim, you validate that part of you. But it's important to not stay there for too long. It can take you into a black hole, which is not the most useful part of the healing process. It's not where your growth lies. Feeling your pain initially brings to the surface a lot of negative emotions. It can sometimes be too much to handle, but it's important to get it all out because if you let it fester inside you, it will only lead to more pain.

Use those negative emotions wisely. No one wants to feel the negative emotions, but these negative emotions are our teachers. Peel the layers and do a deep-dive analysis of what these negative emotions are really telling you. Anger, for example, is saying that you deserved better, bitterness is saying that you need better, jealousy is showing you that you can have better. None of these are pleasant, but it's important to understand that they are all part of the healing process and are absolutely essential.

One of the key things to understand during this process is that if your anger or bitterness is targeted towards certain individuals that you feel caused you pain, remember that hurt people hurt people. Only if we are hurt or are in pain ourselves, will we cause more pain and hurt to others. It's not easy, because you always expect better from others, but this acknowledgment of the rawness of life will help put things a little more in perspective and will also help you be kinder.

After we let ourselves feel the pain for long enough, it does many things. A part of us feels validated—we are no

50

longer carrying the burden of bitterness inside of us, and we also start to feel lighter. We give ourselves permission to understand the root causes of our pain so we can feel something different and something other than the pain itself.

Feeling the pain is really healing the pain. It goes hand in hand. One cannot happen without the other. *"Your task is not to seek for love, but merely to seek and find all the barriers within yourself that you have built against it"* (Rumi). Pain *is* the biggest barrier to love. Only those who are in pain will cause more pain to others. But when you love and feel love, you want to spread more of that. When you feel pain, there is little room for love.

When you let yourself feel the pain to see what caused it, so you can use it to propel you forward to grow instead of holding you back to shrink you, you are feeling pain the right way. You will also be acknowledging parts of you that were carrying the broken dreams of what could have been. You are reliving the dreams you once had, and you are also allowing yourself to become that person, even if for a moment, who had those dreams. And that's exactly your starting point to a whole new version of you. Seeing glimpses of the person that dreamt those dreams in who you are today, is the place from which you will be reborn, and your new reality will be created. When you start feeling more and more like that person who had those dreams, you realize that that person has been within you all along— and is still there somewhere. They were just covered by so much pain that you forgot they existed. And if you keep ignoring the pain, you will keep ignoring the person you always have been at your core. You will keep ignoring the person you can become.

Ironically, feeling the pain gives life back to the deadness, to the numbness that you feel inside, and it helps you put the pieces back together of your broken self. It helps you feel alive again—even though the initial thought of most people is to the contrary.

In our ability to feel, truly lies our power to heal.

8.

I AM ENOUGH

If you've been told for a long time that you are not enough, but deep down you know that that's not true—read this to understand why others may try to project that onto you, and to make sense of how you really feel.

Sometimes we grow up believing that we are either lacking something or that we're not enough—not good enough, smart enough, beautiful enough, capable enough. I'm not sure how this started and when. It's almost as if there were some imaginary societal standard for what "enough" was, and we were all measured against that. Who defined that standard, and what was used as a measure for it? That is still unknown. We are each individuals in our own right, meant to grow and shine in our own ways and at our own pace; yet we want to know how we perform against each other at different points in time. This is often projected onto us by others, and we tend to internalize it over time, until it becomes a part of our own voice, our own experience, a part of our own being. But I wonder why some people try projecting this on others, even though we ourselves know deep down that we are actually enough?

Are they just projecting their own insecurities and fears on us, or maybe those of the ones around them? They may be looking at us and our lives from the lens of their own past failures and current disappointments. They might draw limits on what we are capable of, limits on who we should be and what we can do; not because they understand our potential, but because it somehow matches their perception of us. Some people like putting others in a box, placing them within defined limits—not because we ask for those definitions, but because it would help them understand others better. Putting others in a box suits some because they fear what others' potential will reveal about their own shortcomings. Some of them fear the unknown and the uncertainty life has to offer. But what they forget is that some of us are best left undefined. For some of us, our potential is limitless, and *we are undefinable.*

We should not give up based on what "they" say—they have not been with us on our journey, they don't understand who we are and what makes us tick. They have not fought our battles, overcome our fears, seen our scars and wounds. So why would we give them enough importance to devalue who we are, what we're capable of, and our whole journey? We meet such individuals throughout our lives, people who have not been with us on the days when we thought we weren't enough and fought hard to prove ourselves wrong. They have not seen us on our days when we were going to give up on ourselves but found the strength to give ourselves just one more chance. We placed all the bets on ourselves and have come out stronger than before, and now know deep down that we are actually enough. More than enough. Because we get to decide for ourselves what "enough" really is. We get to tell ourselves that our past experiences are enough, and that our scars and wounds have taught us enough. We've scaled the mountains, not merely showing others what that's like, but building it brick by brick until the foundation feels strong enough for us to build our characters on.

I am here to tell you that no matter what you were told growing up or in the past, *you are enough*. Don't look at anyone else, but ask yourself how you really feel. When you look at your past, do you merely see mistakes, or do you see strength and power through those mistakes? Have you found a way of covering your scars and wounds with enough love and kindness that nothing else can seep through? Through your deepest fears and insecurities, have you found your greatest courage?

We are not flaky or fickle-minded anymore—our thoughts, words, and actions finally align. We are not disturbed by the noise around us anymore, nor are we questioning our own worth. We are not wondering if we are enough based on the love and kindness we receive from others, because we know that the love and kindness they give to the world is a reflection of what's inside them.

When we look around at everyone else and all there is, I know that the only one we need to be better than is the person we were yesterday. The only voice we need to listen to is our own, and my voice is finally telling me that I am enough. I have enough strength, enough courage, enough intelligence. I am finally good enough, for me. And that's more than enough.

9.

HINDSIGHT

When you've been wired to think that looking back will not serve you, this gives you a reason to look back so you can understand how far you've come.

When we're adulting in full-steam mode, keeping up with our day-to-day responsibilities, juggling life and its many demands, our time becomes very limited. Our days are blocked into chunks of hours, going from one task to the other, checking off everything we have on our to-do lists. Sometimes it feels like we're not just wearing many different hats in a day, but living many different lives altogether. We become who we need to become when we need to become so that we can keep this ship of life afloat. Our days can feel intense as we go through the motions of our tasks. We try to deal with all of our emotions along the way and hardly have enough hours to get it all done—let alone some spare time for reflection—not just of our current lives, but also our past.

It takes a whole lot of courage on our side to look back on our lives and understand the parts of the equation that sums up to who we are today. We are looking at our past selves through the lens of who we are today, what we are today, and where we are today. Evaluating our journey and all the detours, thinking about the *coulda, woulda, shouldas* of life. Did we make the right choices at the right times? What exactly were we thinking when we made a specific choice? Who were we back then when we wanted a certain life path? It is never easy for our now-evolved selves to look back on our life and see the person we used to be, recalling the missteps and the person who made them. It takes a lot of self-forgiveness to be able to look at that person and understand that we did our best in those moments—but also know today that we can make different choices going forward.

Who knew that a simple act of looking back carries the power to weave the story of our lives? If we don't ever look back, how do we understand how far we've come and how much we've overcome? What would we use as a yardstick to measure our own progress and growth over time, if not for the bits and pieces from our past that we can best remember? There has to be a starting point that we can pinpoint in our past that made us move a certain way, choose a certain direction. From that place we can trace who we have evolved into and how the choices we made have helped us reach where we are.

Many people think that looking back on your life is not a great idea. While I agree that harping over the past may not be the best, I think there's great wisdom in understanding the story our lives. It helps us connect the dots for where we are headed, using where we are right now as a bridge. Looking at the past and evaluating where we are today helps us put things in perspective. What may have seemed doubtful back then has truly evolved into a good choice that we are able to see now. Something that felt like a question in the past has found its answers in our lives in today's time. Maybe our past mistakes were not mistakes after all; maybe they were really the steppingstones to where we are now. We were influenced so much by the circumstances of our lives and surroundings back then, that we were unable to look with fresh eyes and clarity to be able to see all the possibilities that lie ahead. It is only when we look back that can we make full sense of our present; this is true not only of our lives, but when we look at others' lives too.

We can use our past as our starting point, as a guide, as a checkpoint. Did we really accomplish all that we set out to, or did we let other things get in the way of our dreams? Do we feel how we thought we would about our lives today? Did all our hard work pay off as much as we thought it would? When we look back on our lives, we don't just see random occurrences; what we actually see is the connection to our future.

Without looking back to see how all the events played out and how they influence our lives today, how do we sum them all up to equal a whole?

10.

TAKE A DEEP BREATH

If you are feeling overwhelmed and need a little nudge just to get started.

Take a deep breath, or a few breaths.

When you feel exhausted and are wondering what's the point and where all of this will lead.
   When you have a long to-do list, but don't know where to start.
   When you don't want to move forward with the week, but have to.
   When you don't feel like showing up, but need to.

   When you think you're done and realize this was only the beginning.
   When you don't get what you signed up for.
   When you have a deep desire to accomplish something, but just don't know where to begin.
   Where you feel like giving up, but there's a flicker of light inside you telling you not to.

   Take a breath when you don't know what the right thing to do is.

   Take a breath when you're not sure how you're going to make it, but you just know that you owe it to yourself.

   Take a breath when the world wants you to believe that the best is behind you, but you know that it's not true.

Take a breath when most people around you have given up on you, but you have not given up on yourself.

Take a breath when you know that what seems like the end of the road is just a bend.

Take a breath when you feel overwhelmed but need to move on anyway.

And once you have cracked the code on how to begin, how to move forward, take some more deep breaths just so you can calm your mind when there's way too much going on.

Take a few more deep breaths just so you can feel the calmness spread through your system.

Take a few more deep breaths just so you can feel this new life become your current reality.

Take a few more deep breaths as you adjust to this new version of yourself, this new idea of the life you want to create.

Take a few deep breaths as you let yourself sink into the depths of your new reality.

Take a few deep breaths as you hold more space between yourself and your dreams, as you create an expanse where your dreams cannot just survive, but thrive.

Take a few more deep breaths as you grow into the idea of who you want to become as you feel more and more centered and your center now becomes your anchor.

Take a few more deep breaths as you put the past behind you and focus more on the present and the future you want, as you ground yourself in the new reality of your dreams.

Take a few more deep breaths as you let yourself just be.

Take a few more deep breaths as you feel the sunshine on your face, as you let yourself enjoy long walks in nature.

Take a few more deep breaths as you let yourself rise above your wildest thoughts and dreams.

Take a few more deep breaths as you let your crazy self dream crazy dreams some more.

Take a few more deep breaths as you let yourself just breathe.

Take a few more deep breaths as you let yourself rise above your fears and dare to dream what you want to dream.

Take a few more deep breaths as you let yourself just be.

Take a few more deep breaths as you listen to the beating of your own heart.

Take a few more deep breaths as you see the anxiety slip away.

Take a few more deep breaths as you see your worries wipe away.

Take a few more deep breaths as you settle into a new reality, that you once only dreamed of.

Take a few more deep breaths as you let yourself enjoy the success of all your hard work, without worrying that it will be taken away from you.

Take a few more deep breaths as you let yourself get

more and more comfortable in your skin, with who you are becoming—uncertain of what that might look like.

Take a few more deep breaths as you let yourself look back somewhat at your past—at the hurt, at the pain—without it having its pull on you anymore.

Take a few more deep breaths as you think of all the dreams you used to have, that you somehow over the course of your life decided to shelf away.

Take a few more deep breaths as you let yourself believe what you might become.

Take a few more deep breaths as you let yourself believe what might just be possible for you too.

Take a few more breaths as you find the strength to reopen that box of dreams you once had.

Take a few more breaths as you find the courage to not just open that box of dreams you had, but also the courage to believe that there's still hope.

Take a few more breaths as you believe that what once might have been an uncomfortable reality is now a distant speck in the vastness of joy, hope, and profound love that your life now encompasses.

Take a few more breaths to realize you are now not just dreaming of a life you wish, but living that life you once wished for.

Take a few more breaths to realize that you are now the person you once wished for.

Take a few more breaths to realize that you can become more than what you once hoped for.

And if you need more reasons, take some more breaths to realize that life can be more beautiful than we ever imagined, if only we let ourselves. Life can be even more precious than we once wished for, just more than we ever imagined possible for us.

Many times, it is in these small breaths that our lives can be changed forever. It is in the depths of these small breaths that our lives and futures can be loved and grown. It is in these small breaths that so much distance can be created between where we are now and where we want to be—that this distance actually provides us the space to grow and become who we need to become in order to accomplish what we need to.

Don't ever underestimate the power of these small breaths and the gift they can give you.

PART TWO

MOVE,
When You
Are Ready
for Change

11.

ON FINDING A WAY
BACK TO YOURSELF

When you are ready to move forward with your life, start by looking inward.

After taking the time to pause and reflect on where we are in life and which direction we want to go in, many of us try to become better versions of who we've been or create a new version of ourselves altogether. There is a good chance that we might not know where to begin this journey, and we could also stumble many times throughout. Sometimes all it may take is remembering who we were right at the beginning; other times we must find a completely different path, because nothing else seems to be working. It doesn't matter how much we look outside ourselves to find the answers to our current questions or to the ones that life itself has in store for us. When we have reflected enough on where we are in life and know that we're ready for change, the best place to start is often by *looking within*.

Instead, many of us tend to look outside ourselves a lot—at others, at life circumstances, at past events—to figure out where our moral compass is pointing or where our internal GPS is going. We look to others to see if the molds that they are creating for their own lives could help shape the lives that we are looking for. When we're feeling lost, it's very easy to want to look outside to come up with definitions for what could fit into our own lives. But the ironic thing is that the more we look outside ourselves long-term, the more lost we will feel. Looking at others' lives could give us some sort of initial guidance or direction, but that will eventually wear off. No matter how much we look to others' lives for their ways of living, for their definitions of happiness, success, joy, courage—nothing will fit as well as the ones we come up with for our own lives because our journeys are all not the same. No matter how much we try to seek validation for where we are in life or where we're supposed to be, nothing outside of us will give us any of these answers. No matter how much of a people pleaser we've been and continue to be, it will not serve us any more than it already has. The answers and validation and confirmations we look for are not outside us; they always have been, and will be, inside us.

It's not going to be an easy path, coming up with our own definitions in life, especially if it's not something that we're used to doing. Irrespective of what our past had in store and what we've done with it, we must know that we have a choice in front of us every single day. Thinking about what we would like our lives to look like and what we would like to make of them, will become the building blocks for the remainder of our days. That becomes the foundation of our lives. We need to think about what we want our future selves to look like and what kind of virtues we would like to best describe us. What do we want our days to be filled with? What do we want our lives to be defined by, and what do we want our legacy to be? Because whether we like it or not, we are creating our legacies by merely living this life. Whether we're existing, surviving, or thriving, we're telling a story each day through our actions and our words. Through our wins and our losses, through our love and hate, through our joy and sadness. Through our courage and hope.

We may even find ourselves falling many times throughout this process, sometimes wondering who we are to find our own answers to these tough questions in life. But what we need to remember then is that our life is not a constant race of mini-destinations we all need to arrive at and keep up with. There is no podium waiting for us at the end of this journey to see who is number one, two, and three in this illusionary race we have made our lives to be. Life is actually a summation of each of our experiences that truly make us who we are today—to grow into the people we're meant to be, to learn the lessons along the way, and to journey together on this beautiful path. We are allowed to take up space and take some time to find out what really works for us - what makes us tick, what ignites us, fuels us, lights us up. Just because the journey might be tough, we cannot give up on ourselves, our dreams, and what our lives could really become—what *we* could really become. And it's also not just the monotony of a journey as some of us may think of it; it's the lessons, growth, joy, sadness, regret, accomplishments all along the way that make it what it is. We are allowed to make as many pitstops and detours as we need, until it all starts to align with our own values and emotions.

The various milestones and destinations we all arrive at are by-products of our lives, not the main point and purpose of it. The journey is what makes life worth living, and ultimately what makes up life itself. Think about it this way - when we reach a milestone, how long does the feeling of being at or "arriving" at our destination last? Not very long. But how long does the journey take us to get to where we want to be? A lot longer. *The journey has and will always be the point of life.*

We spend a lot of our time and energy focusing on the end result, forgetting all along how beautiful life itself can be. We need to recognize the beauty that makes reaching each milestone along the way so worth it and so much more amazing. Who told us that life is one linear path that needs to be simple and perfect and amazing all along? Who gave us the impression that that was even possible? We're not mere robots meant to live life each day going from one emotion to the other. Life is not just meant to be full of ups and full of experiences leaving us starry-eyed. What is so innately wrong with the misgivings of life and the beautiful imperfections of it all?

Some of us spend hours browsing through our favorite destinations to travel, endless amounts of yearning to be someplace else—as if moving ourselves just as we are, mind and all, will make us feel different from how we do now. Sometimes we go chasing after obscure things that make it seem like they are what life is meant to be about, not understanding that there's way more to life than just being happy all the time. Instead of trying to align our lives to some imaginary standards based on other people's timelines, and failing along the way, it's probably time to rethink what we have pictured for life itself and letting things be so we can just enjoy our own journey and all that it has to offer for a change.

For all we know, maybe this is what life's about and we've been chasing all the wrong things by looking outside ourselves all along.

12.

WHEN YOU'VE
HIT A WALL

When you've gone through the ups and downs
of life to get to where you are, but suddenly
feel like you can't move any further.

When we have reached the point in our lives where the cost of holding back is way more than the price of moving forward, we choose to finally bet on ourselves. We realize we have been living half-lives up until now, and we were suffocating ourselves by inhibiting our own growth. Living in denial of what we are really capable of, of what our full potential is. Somewhere, deep down, afraid of what all this growth and moving forward will uncover, will unleash.

We tell ourselves no more excuses from now on. We don't want to stand by anymore, to be a passenger to other people's lives. We're not observing or passively living anymore; we finally feel in control of our own lives. The past versions of ourselves feel outdated, and we want to leave that person behind so we can move forward in the direction of our calling, which has needed our attention for a long time. We learn to remove all of the mental blocks along the way that kept us where we were, urging us to stay stuck, to just remain where it feels comfortable and familiar. We feel that this was the biggest hurdle to clear the path to get us to where we want to go. We think that we have ultimately conquered the world after fighting the battles to convince ourselves that we are worth it, that we can do it, that great things can be in store for us too. We feel we have scaled the biggest mountain we needed to get to the top. Or so we thought.

We start off with the initial excitement that doing new things brings, along with the pent-up boldness and courage within that we finally choose to bring out into the world. We finally feel confident enough to let our best selves shine through and are vulnerable enough to be able to start something new. We learn to move forward, building piece by piece our path toward the life of our dreams. We put blinders on and do as we need to, lunging forward full-steam until we run into some roadblocks and feel like we are running out of gas. We seem to be trying and trying, and we either hit the same roadblocks or feel like we find ourselves moving in circles, unable to rise up and see if any of this would ultimately materialize into what we're hoping for. We think we've tried enough, but we seem to be getting the same results. Nothing new comes of any of this. It gets hard then. We second-guess every move, we forget the point of it all. Clarity is replaced by intense fog, and everything seems to be blurred.

How do we really move forward, then?

Remember why you started in the first place. That inkling, that thought, that dream. Whether as a fifteen year old, or a twenty-five year old, something in you made you believe that it was possible... for you. For once, you chose to place the bets on yourself. As hard as life can be, you knew that this was your one chance to feel alive. To come alive. To feel whole, purposeful. You had ideas that became fully formed thoughts, and you figured out a path to make them into tangible actions and, therefore, a living reality. All of these steps took immense courage on your end to make it happen. To bring it to life.

We all have our purposes in life, what we think we're meant to do, who we're meant to be. When we know what that is, it's clear. It feels good to just be doing it. It feels peaceful and calming. It feels right. But it's not always going to be an easy path. Some roads and curves will be easier to navigate and maneuver, and sometimes you think you've just hit a wall! Walls are obstacles, and there may be times when there's no way around them. The only way out is to go over them. It may seem hard in the beginning, impossible even. You can't see over the horizon; you don't know if there is a way out. What if it was all just a waste up until now? What if everything will just in the end amount to... nothing? But the most fulfilling things in life, dreams in life, feel this way in the beginning. Most dreams seem too farfetched in the beginning; most goals seem unattainable at the start.

We can give up when we think we've tried it all and the effort is not worth the result in the end. And that's fine too. And then there are times when we know we just owe it to ourselves. We owe it to the fifteen year old who always knew that there's so much more to life than the "tough battles." We owe it to the dreams we dared to dream when no one thought any of that was remotely possible. We owe it to the hopes that fulfilling these dreams would give to million others just like them, who dared to dream dreams that were too big for where they came from.

What would happen to all of these things if we just decided to stop when we hit a wall? Would we feel like we did ourselves justice, or were honest about how much was too much, if enough was truly enough? Maybe, in the end, we would wonder if we were just too jaded. And then we would try to understand what really made us so okay with the idea of giving up.

13.

LEAN *INTO* YOUR DISCOMFORT

The discomfort you've been feeling is not a bad thing. It's trying to tell you something; you just have to listen to it.

How often do we reach that tipping point to make a big change in our lives… and just stop? It could be a dream, an opportunity, or a circumstance we find ourselves in the midst of. We know we want to move forward, but something keeps holding us back. We're not sure if it's the familiarity and comfort of old patterns or the fear of the new lightness we may find. We try half-heartedly and nothing seems to change. Things stay stagnant; they remain the same.

We become too afraid to move forward, too scared of the unknown, too fearful of what all might change if we change. Will we be as successful as we want, and will we have the same people around us we once knew? Will all of the love and happiness still be there? We think about the ripple effect if we move too much too soon. What would be the impact of our actions, not just on us, but the world around us? Will it all still be the same? We get caught up in our own thoughts and questions, only to find ourselves just standing still.

We start to wonder what's wrong with the life we now have that makes us want more. Are we missing something? The truth is, there does not have to be something wrong with what we currently have for us to want more—and there's nothing wrong with wanting more while fully being happy with what we currently have, either. They're not mutually exclusive. We don't have to despise our lives currently if we are craving for more.

They can coexist - loving what we have, yet wanting more.

All we're doing is leaning into our discomfort—that little voice urging us to see that there's more to life. That little feeling inside telling us that we can be more, we can have more, if only we're willing to step away from life as we know it just for a little bit so we may be able to see what lies ahead.

They say, *magic happens when you decide to step out of your comfort zone.* But what does that mean for us in our own lives? And is it even possible for us? Our comfort zone is our life as we currently know it, the life that we have built for ourselves. Our past and our present that has made up all the beautiful things we have become a part of, overcoming all our fears and rejections. It's the safety in the love of all the people around us. It's the safety in the joy of all the moments that make us, take us, and carry us forward. To even think of stepping away from it, outside of it, means there's a part of us that will have to start all over again. Maybe our entire being will have to restart all over again, which also means we don't start from a place of known, but unknown.

The thing we tend to often forget is that when we step out of our comfort zone, we never really start from scratch all over again. We think we do, but we actually don't. Even though we step away from our comfort zone, our starting point is who we are today. It's who we have already become. It's who we have built ourselves to be from all our past experiences put together. So our baseline of starting from scratch is different today than it was a few years ago, something simple we all often forget. And I think that this is one of the biggest barriers preventing us from stepping out of our comfort zone—this misapprehension of the concept of our baseline today. Maybe it's the fear of reliving how it felt when we really did start from scratch when we were younger, more inexperienced. But having gone through those challenges and having been resilient through those has toughened us, made us stronger in understanding who we are today, what we want from our lives, and where we want to go now.

Often, our immediate reaction to that discomfort telling us to step out of our comfort zone, is to ignore it. In the midst of meetings, appointments, social gatherings, that discomfort in our gut is probably the first thing to be ignored. We may even have to schedule some time in our calendar to be able to assess it, evaluate it, dissect it, to understand what it's really trying to tell us. It's something we don't even have a name for, a slight feeling that's just *lingering*, at the back of our minds and stomachs, as we go through the routine of each day. What if we find something we don't know how to deal with? **But today I ask you to lean into that discomfort—you have so much more to gain than you realize.**

14.

ON FINDING WHAT YOU LOVE DOING

When you've been searching for what makes
you come alive and have still not found it, read
this to move you just a bit closer to where you
want to go.

Many of us look for things in life that leave us feeling energized, rejuvenated, lighter than we were before. We sometimes look for these in the people we meet or in the things we do in life. There are instances when we spend time with some people and are left with a sense of rejuvenation; then there are others with whom we feel mentally exhausted. Similarly, there are things in life that we all do that leave us in such emotional states.

We often see people around us looking for things in life that they "love" doing, things that make them come alive, that make time slow down for a bit, and that make all the obstacles along the way worth it. We're all searching for this elusive concept in some way or the other, but we don't always know how to go about finding it.

And that can get tricky.

In today's day and age when we have so many options in front of us—not just with the rapidly changing times but also with the evolved technology—how does one pick one of these things over the thousands of other options available to us? There is no navigation system helping us through the myriad emotions we feel during this soul-searching endeavor, nor do we have a guide directing us on which path to take. How is one to know which fork in the road leads us to our destination? After a while, they can all seem like they fit, like they're all things we would like to do. Or it can go to the other extreme, where it feels like the complete opposite—where nothing seems exciting or engaging enough to hold our attention for long.

What we all are probably looking for is some kind of foolproof method to tell us how to get from where we are today to where we want to be; but that bridge can be a rickety old one, and the only way to get on and down from it safely is by listening to our own voice, listening to our heart, and what they are trying to tell us. We will have to find a way of using our own emotional compass to guide us, but for that to happen, we first must learn to be in sync with it. We have to learn to trust it. We need some kind of gut check or emotional response that we can rely on to help us navigate the chaotic waters and the storms during this time.

But how do we even know where to start this search, let alone decide on just one path?

One of the places we can start is by simply being honest with ourselves about what brings us real joy, and not putting any limitations on ourselves. Finding what we love comes less from searching and thinking, and more from searching and doing. *Thinking does not equal doing. Thinking does not equal finding. Thinking does not equal living.*

Loving what you do has so many meanings for different people, and there are so many reasons why people seek this in their lives. Some learned to follow their hearts early in life and have the courage to do so, while others spend years in meaningless jobs until they feel their lives being sucked out of their bodies altogether.

Loving what you do does not make work feel like work, they say. Think about how your seventy-year-old self would feel when they looked back at their life and took stock of each decade. The carefree twenties, responsible thirties, intentional forties and fifties, and near-retirement sixties. What's one wish you had that could leave you with regret, knowing that you could have done more? Something you wish you'd tried harder at, given yourself more chances, pushed just a little bit more to see where it may have taken you? It could be relating to a person, a relationship, a job, a city, a move, a passion… if only you'd given yourself a real chance at it, what would life look like today? What would the remainder of your days and decades have looked like?

That's your answer, at least for now. That's the thing you start with. Let doing that thing—and the feeling it leaves you with—guide you on. Take it one step at a time, one day at a time. Don't ignore that thing, don't ignore that voice, don't ignore that feeling—however small or big they might be—because those are your inherent guides. Those are our inner voices telling us something, only if we're willing to pay enough attention to them and listen. Often, we tend to ignore that voice because we don't really understand it or don't know if it will lead us anywhere. But the more we pay attention to this voice and take it day by day, the more we keep building on a feeling that was once unknown but now feels more familiar. Oddly, it will feel like coming home—like you've waited your whole life and have known this feeling all along, except it was buried under layers of conditioning around who you should be, what you can do, what's expected of you.

It will feel like a familiar space, one you might even feel like you've been in before. It will feel like peace, happiness, and contentment all rolled into one giant block, and from there you will feel like you don't need to look further. Because the funny thing is, you've been looking for answers around you all along to guide you—when it's the questions inside you that needed listening to. You've been looking at others and what they do for clues, when your heart knew all along.

This is your purpose in life, this is your calling.

When we do find what it is we love doing, we must find a way of sticking with it. Finding what we love doing is often not a simple path of going from point A to point B. We are bound to face struggles, obstacles, doubts, fears, and insecurities along the way—sometimes to the point where we wonder if it is all worth it and if it's even meant to be. But whenever we do find what it is we love doing, we will feel rooted. Like we belong. It will feel like we have nothing left to prove to anyone anymore, simply because we have come into our own and have found ourselves in the process of finding what it is we love doing.

We will feel grounded; deep in our core we start putting the pieces together and start feeling whole again. Bit by bit, day by day. As we keep stringing these pieces together, we will start to feel complete. In a way that no love or relationship has ever made us feel until now. It will feel like our heart, mind, and soul are in alignment, and it will feel like the search has finally stopped. It will feel like we have arrived where we were always meant to be, and always knew deep down where we wanted to go. It will feel like love—the kind we give to ourselves. We start taking better care of ourselves and our soul feels alive, knowing that this is what it was meant to do in this lifetime. It's a gift, one that no one can give to you—only one that you can give to yourself. And one that you will thank yourself for later in life.

You will not be the one who is older and has regrets, but the one who will stand proud for taking that chance on yourself when you could. You will thank yourself for making the time to stick with your search, your persistence to continue on that path, and the courage to follow your heart. The choices you make today will in fact define your future. The path you take today will in fact lead you to newer destinations. Your journey today will decide your happiness tomorrow.

I hope you have the courage and are bold enough to ask yourself all the questions you need to, irrespective of if you will find the answers or not; because sometimes the ground-breaking ideas and perspectives lie not in the answers, but in the questions themselves. When we ask ourselves the life-altering questions, we start to get on the path of our search. When we ask ourselves the tough questions, we seek to find the truth that would satiate these questions just for a little bit. Asking ourselves questions means we are willing to unlearn what we know and are willing to understand that life as we know it may not always be enough.

And that's half the battle.

Understanding that we can want more, be more, ask for more means that we are willing to change, to evolve, and to grow. It also means that we need to get out of our comfort zones and sit with the feeling of discomfort for a while. Change often takes time, however big or small it might be. But the longer we are willing to stick with it, to ask the right questions, the deeper the impact of this will be. Getting comfortable with the idea of discomfort and change is often where most of our growth lies. And in our growth and honesty with ourselves lies our freedom to understand what it is that we truly love and what it is that we truly want. You will be willing to scale as many mountains, overcome as many obstacles as necessary because there is nothing else in the world that makes you feel like finding your calling does. It not only feels right and like it fits, it also feels like finding it itself is the answer.

The questions will stop, and the answers rise. Or the questions will remain, and you will be okay with that. You will find courage in times you didn't think you could, you will find joy in the smallest of victories, you will know you have found what you love because it's not always the end result that will matter. There will be enough joy in the act of doing itself, that whatever the end result is won't really matter at all. Because it's not just the destination that's important, but the joy of the journey itself. You will know you have found what you love, because the thoughts just don't stop, there is a constant voice inside you telling you to nudge forward in that direction.

It might feel illogical and scary sometimes— but when has the greatest love ever been logical?

15.

YOU WIN SOME,
YOU LOSE SOME

*If you're trying to find some balance in life,
read this to understand what you should keep
and what you should let go.*

Even though I would like to say that the hardest part is now behind you, that you've won all your battles fair and square so you can now live happily ever after, that may not fully be the truth.

It has indeed been a long journey to understand what you want from your life and to figure out who you want to become to get there. You know the number of times you've had to pick yourself back up to remind yourself that there's more to life, you know the number of times you wished for the darkness to just fade away, you know how many people you've had to prove wrong along the way. You are aware of the number of times you've had to scrape right to the bottom just to be able to show up each day; and as hard as it was at times, you've stayed consistent. You've done all the right things, and you've become stronger than you ever were before.

However, reaching this point of knowing what you want to do with your life and convincing your mind to understand this as a possibility is only half your battle. Even though you've made it this far, you're becoming the person you're meant to be, and you want to dive right into the life you're trying to create, you will still have to make plenty of decisions along the way. Even though it feels like this particular phase of your journey has been the toughest and has lasted the longest, it's still only one phase of your entire journey. There's a long way to go until you reach the end, and there will be times throughout where you are still going to have to make some important choices.

Some easy, some difficult. Some obvious, some not so obvious. There's going to be a trade-off each time you are moving towards your goal, and you are going to have to decide what is worth it and what isn't. You are going to have to make choices where you see some things falling apart, while others are coming together. Some are breaking off to never come back, while some stick around to become better. For some it's just a pause; for others, it's the end.

You simply can't have it all.

We will have to be ready for the times we're at a fork in the road, where we will have to lose some things in order for us to accomplish some more things in life. Even though you are sure of the road ahead of you, there will be plenty of tiny obstacles along the way you will need to overcome to reach the end. But remember that as long as you are taking steps slowly but surely forward, you are moving in the right direction.

There might be different paths that we may not have been able to see before, which become obvious now. There may be different ways of getting things done that seem clearer now. We might have been looking at life and the future with one lens; now it might be time to change things up a little. Maybe we don't always need to dive right into our goals head-on, but we can ease into the business of living out our dreams. Maybe we don't always need to decide the pace we want to move at, but let the pace decide itself for a change. Maybe we don't always have to pack every weekend with things to do, places to be, and people to see, but we can instead surrender to the journey ahead and see where it takes us. We don't always have to look at everything as one-dimensional, but can start looking at things with the richness that living life deeply can bring. We can start allowing ourselves to feel the moments and the little joys that come with it for a change, instead of letting our minds be occupied with anxiety and worry. We can keep letting ourselves get out of our comfort zones to see what we're capable of doing and achieving, instead of still holding ourselves back and letting all our potential just stack up on top of each other.

Holding ourselves back is only going to make us feel more frustrated. Maybe it's time to start letting go, just a little bit, and see what lies ahead for us. We can live in peace for once knowing that we have finally found what we've been looking for all this while. It can feel different, unusual even. Because this is probably not what you're used to, not how you've been living life. But let that feeling soak in. If you have worked hard to reach this far, you are allowed to revel in this in-between phase of your life—after you have found what you love doing by becoming the person you are meant to be, and before you dive right into the life you want to create. You are allowed to create a bit of space to pause, either to just be or to understand how you can fine-tune your moves better. Get some of the finer details squared off.

But we also need to realize that if we want to let more into our lives, we are going to have create a space for it. We will need to lose the comfort of empty spaces so they can be occupied by more opportunities to fill into our lives. We will need to lose some of our extra time if we want to make our dreams come true. We are going to have to sacrifice meeting people if we're trying to befriend ourselves first. We might need to trade going out for staying in. Something's just got to give while we are trying to live out our dreams and accomplish our goals. We are going to have to be more mindful and intentional with our choices and our lives. We may even have to lose some of our rigidity if we're trying to let the flow into our lives.

No matter the path we choose and how we choose it, we can be certain that some choices are going to be ahead of us that we need to prepare ourselves for.

To finally rise above the horizon, we will have to make the choice to be prepared to take that long trek.

16.

AN EMPTY CUP

When you feel you are on the brink of a burnout, read this to understand why that's actually the opposite of how you should be living.

An empty cup serves no one.

If you have lived life with the mindset that you must be running on fumes in order to stop and refill your tank, you may have already gone too far. You may not be at the point of no return yet, but it might be a little late for you to retrace your steps and make different choices to *not* reach the stage where you've run out of gas. You've worked incredibly hard to show that you deserve this life that you are living. You have put others' needs and wants before yours, which society has taught us should be celebrated. But by this point, you're not only completely overworked, but you may have also lost sight of what's truly important to call it a good life.

Our cultures have glorified having an empty cup and reaching the point of burnout for so long that we often think we're doing the right thing by taking care of others before ourselves. Sometimes we forget that if we can't thrive ourselves, how are we going to truly help others? We may not be able to see it immediately or visibly, but there are intangible ways that others can break because we haven't been able to fix ourselves first.

Broken pieces of us can lead to broken pieces of others.

What we don't realize is that every event leading up to our burnout is a choice that we make, which we have full control of. We don't always think we do, but in reality, we actually do. Having an empty cup means many occurrences of not saying no when you want to, not having proper boundaries, and putting your priorities on the back burner constantly.

But many of these situations can be dealt with in ways we may not have thought of until now. For instance, an overload of work that comes in can be tackled by having conversations with our peers and bosses about expectations. Invitations to go out with friends after a long week can be declined by having discussions about our new priorities and making it clear that it's not personal. Trips with acquaintances can be replaced by a trip with loved ones, focusing on rest and relaxation.

We don't *always* have to do what looks good on the outside to show the world that we are there for them every time they need us. We can be there for people while being there for ourselves too. We can take care of people, while also taking care of ourselves. We can grow in ways that we need and help others grow too. This does not have to be a zero-sum game or mutually exclusive; doing one thing does not have to exclude doing another,

While reaching the point of an empty cup can happen fairly quickly and easily in today's fast-paced world, refilling that cup can honestly take a while. Our cups can become empty in a matter of weeks or months depending on how much we have on our plates, but refilling that cup could take years. We probably don't even recognize we are running on fumes until we are snapped back into reality by an intervention of some sort. It could happen by external events not in our control, but it could also happen by constant changes in behavior with our loved ones. We snap more than we usually do, we psychoanalyze everything and everyone around us, we are constantly on alert to understand the waves of reality shifting around us. None of this is normal behavior, none of these are us operating under normal circumstances to reach normal results. Our lives start shifting little by little, and we wonder how all this happened to us. One project at work led to many projects, one dinner invitation led to many more, one weekend led to many weekends rolled in. The truth is that while we were going through the motions of building these incredibly busy lives, we inherently knew that this was not sustainable in the long-term. But we were so short-sighted in the moment, wanting to accomplish our goals or gain instant gratification, that we lost sight of the reality of our lives and reality of our true selves. We wanted to be different things to different people at different times; and it seems like we forgot to be what we needed to be for our own selves, first.

The good news is that if we are able to recognize our missteps early enough, we can gain some sort of control back of our lives. You can start by looking at your life and days as blocks of hours and phases. What do you want each of these blocks in a day to look like, and what would you like each phase of your life to represent? Is there a way to incorporate mini-vacations into your days without leaving your home? Can you look at setting up effective morning and evening routines? Can you focus on your health, eating right, and meditating on the daily, so you don't need to plan a big vacation to escape? Think about how you can enhance your life in small and big ways in your everyday. Think about where you can quickly go to regain your direction back to the center of your core, so you don't have to find yourself in a position again where you have lost all sense of direction in life. There are times where all we need is a good dinner out, some champagne, and a bubble bath. But there are times when even a vacation does not take away the blues of our lives. What do we do then, and how do we get back on track?

Journal: One of the most effective techniques to help identify what we are feeling and what we want to do going forward—when our minds feel like a landmine of thoughts—is to journal. You can write all the thoughts on what you are feeling about a situation, how you think you got to where you are, and where you want to go moving forward. Journaling is most effective if it is done every day; particularly when you are dealing with overwhelming thoughts and feelings. Journaling may not be for everyone, though. For those to whom the idea of sitting down with a cup of coffee and writing down all their thoughts is not inviting, maybe think about talking through your thoughts with someone you love. This can be a really effective outlet for your mind.

Start setting boundaries: Boundaries are a controversial topic, depending on which relationships we are discussing. I understand that sometimes we feel obligated to do what needs to be done when duty calls. In this scenario we need to understand which relationships can be set aside, and for how long, depending on how much you think they are contributing to your growth and life in general. If you are feeling more of a drain, then you know it's time to Marie Kondo your closet full of relationships and build a life only with relationships that truly bring you joy. Just as we can declutter our lives of all the material things we possess, we can also apply the same concept and declutter our lives of all the relationships not bringing us joy anymore. Think about your emotional energies and what you think helps enhance them. The "yes" culture for relationships can sometimes go too far, so we need to decide and see what's working for us and what's not.

Find what you love doing: As you get more of an idea of what's causing you to burn out and where you're headed, decluttering your life of relationships not helping you anymore leaves you with a little more time than you originally had. It frees up minutes, hours, and mental space, giving you a chance to focus on activities that you can use to refuel your overarching sense of purpose in life. It may seem like you are suddenly not living with blinders anymore, or not living life with the sense of attachment that you need to always be doing things for others. It will be liberating. And every activity that you add to your tank of things you love doing, also adds back more to your life to make it feel fuller than it did before.

Surround yourself with good energies: We are as good as the people we surround ourselves with. When we are not spending time at work or at home with our families, we are choosing to spend it with other people. And the quality of these individuals is going to directly reflect on the outcomes of our lives. We don't need to be around people who don't have good intentions toward us or wish us well. As much as we feel like we need to have other people in our lives to celebrate the good times with, I'm here to tell you that quality is more important than quantity. Sometimes, absence or lack is better than the presence of a few who don't want the best for you. Don't misunderstand frenemies for friends. There's a difference.

Love yourself some more each day: As much as we can surround ourselves with love, the biggest love we will always need in life—irrespective of what we can get externally—is our own love. The more we learn to love ourselves and our lives, the more we can love those around us. The more we can learn to be friends with ourselves, the more friends we can make. The more we function with a clean and pure heart, the more it reflects in everything else that we do. The ripple effect of self-love is not just seen but also felt by everyone around us; and each one is going to want a sprinkle of your magic dust on them.

17.

OUTGROWN SPACES

*When you've outgrown the spaces you
once yearned to be in.*

nherently, we wish to be a part of something greater than ourselves. A place or a set of people that makes where we live feel like home, a place less lonely with them in it, where we're looking out for one another and where we find meaning. Where we seek the truth of who we are as individuals and what we can collectively bring to each other's lives. Many of us seek that belonging, yearn for that feeling. But where do people find belonging? It's one of our most basic needs as humans, yet many of us find it increasingly difficult—especially in today's ever-changing world.

Belonging is a sense of connectedness that we feel as individuals, whether it's to a city, a particular place, or a group of people. Feeling like we belong is a way of finding our own place within the world. We know that we fit in that space—we know that there is a small area in that place carved out just for us, and if we weren't there, that space would be empty. We'd be missed.

Belonging is a familiar feeling—it's not fleeting. Having a strong sense of belonging helps us feel grounded. Even during times when everything around us is changing, we are still able to find and keep our place within the larger scheme of things. It makes us feel a bit safer than before; it makes us feel more secure. There is no one path when it comes to belonging, there is no correct way of doing things to find belonging, and there is no right or wrong when it comes to belonging. Some find belonging with people, and some in solitude. Some find it in music, and some in cooking. Some find it in places, and some find it within the people in those places. For some of us belonging comes easily, and for some it may take a while.

As we continue our journeys of discovering who we are as individuals, we tend to sense a constant evolution happening within us. There might come a time when we feel like where we once belonged can change. We feel like we may have outgrown that space, the space we once yearned to be a part of. It is not a one-time event, but a small drift that starts with unintentional smaller events that all eventually seem to add up. The change may have been happening for a while, but it may take some sort of tipping point for us to realize this. Things don't feel right anymore. You don't feel loved the way you want to; you don't feel seen the way you deserve.

You feel like you just don't fit in any longer. Not because the space is too large for you or something you can't be a part of, but because it has become a space where you feel you need to shrink who you are (or are meant to be) if you want to be a part of it. It seems to come at the cost of you losing yourself bit by bit, or having to betray pieces of yourself, who you're meant to be, just so you can belong. The change may have been so gradual that it took time to even understand this phenomenon happening within. And even when you do identify this, accepting that you don't belong where you used to can be hard. It can take some time to reach that place and to understand that things are not the same anymore, that you are not who you used to be, and that you don't want to be who you've been.

Change is the only constant in life, but growth is a variable. When we do grow, there is a period of time—a middle ground—when we don't fit into our old spaces anymore, but we don't quite know our new ways yet, either. It can be a lonely time, when you feel like you are wandering alone for a while just so you can figure it all out.

You know you want to be a part of something greater than yourself, but you also know that you yourself are meant to be great. It's a weird dichotomy you find yourself in - one side of you is pushing to move ahead, while the other side is pulling you to hold back—asking you to shine less, sing a bit softer, dance a bit slower. Change who you are at your core so you can morph into what others think of you—and then you'd belong.

But our hearts don't feel light anymore in those spaces, instead they are occupied with anxiety. Our soul is not at ease anymore, instead we're left with an uncomfortable feeling. The lightness in us is replaced with a heaviness that we can't seem to figure out or quite put words to or understand. But it's all just there. The heaviness, the discomfort, the weighing down.

You know in your heart you've outgrown that space, but your mind tries telling you otherwise. That you need them, that you should stay—we all feel like we should be liked by everyone. Invariably, there comes a time when the cost of fitting in is too much and may come at the price of our own growth or happiness. And sometimes the way we pay that price is by shrinking ourselves and limiting our beliefs of what we can and cannot accomplish, what we're worth and capable of doing. There will come a time then, when we must ask ourselves the question: How much is too much? And is it all worth it?

Do we continue on that way just so we can fit in or should we be strong enough to carve our own path and wander alone for a bit just so we can feel like we belong... to ourselves? There may come a time when we must choose between fitting in or belonging to ourselves, and I hope you choose you.

Moving on.

Move on from spaces in which you feel like you don't belong anymore. Move on from clothes that don't represent you anymore. Move on from things you don't feel for anymore. Move on from ideas not serving you anymore. Move on from people not helping you move forward anymore. Move on when you have been giving yourself more reasons to stay than you should be.

Life is too short to refit, to re-feel things we have long outgrown. The more you hold on to what is not meant for you anymore, the more you hold yourself back from what can be—a space to find more beautiful people, words, and places. Where you don't just fit in easily, but also where you feel like you truly belong.

18.

LOSING MAY NOT
BE A LOSS

If you feel like you are losing who you used to be, read this to understand that you are actually gaining a whole new you.

We often associate losing with loss. We look at losing as one-dimensional—from the perspective of what was, but now isn't. What we once had, but now don't, who we once were, but now aren't. But sometimes losing could also actually mean gaining. It may not just be a loss; it could potentially be a win.

When you feel like you are losing a part of yourself, losing who you used to be, it also means that you are now growing newer parts of you that you didn't have before. You may just be getting rid of parts of you that you knew you didn't want a long time ago but were too afraid to let go of. And gaining better parts of yourself that you didn't know you needed to become a part of something larger.

Growth in itself means change, and it can be hard. Especially when you get out of your comfort zone and try something new, you feel like you are losing your old self, and you may not recognize the person you'd become. You probably wonder - If you are not parts of who you've always been, who are you really, then? And growth is not just something that happens within us, but with those around us too. Our relationships are constantly evolving—the relationships we have with ourselves and the relationships we have with others. Our initial reaction to growth or change is almost always to refrain or resist it. The main reason we do this is because we are afraid of losing the known and finding the unknown. We have grown so used to living in the skin we have, that we are petrified of the layers underneath it. We are afraid of letting parts of ourselves go that we have held on to for so long—bits and pieces that we put together through our strengths, challenges, and resilience, that have made us all that we are today. We are afraid of what might remain of us, afraid of who we might become, afraid of what all this would mean for us. Not only for us, but for those around us as well. What impacts will this have, and will we all be able to withstand this change? Maybe what we are afraid of is realizing that there are parts of us we don't need any more and that we could actually come into our own power?

Is this what we are really afraid of?

We seem to love definitions and have always understood life in defined terms. Defining who we are, and identifying who we're becoming—but have we considered that maybe losing a part of ourselves may also mean gaining a whole new identity that we are proud of, or gaining something we didn't even know we were missing? Something that completes us and makes us feel whole.

In our own lives, we are so willing to morph and twist and turn for others who we know are worth it, but I sometimes wonder - what will remain of us in the end? When all is said and done, will we even recognize the person we are anymore? Will too much time have passed and too much change have happened for us to be able to trace our steps, or will we feel like we need to start all over again? Then why are we denying ourselves so many good things in the name of fear, just because we lack the courage to see what's on the other side that could be better for us than what we have today?

What better feeling is there than the feeling of being free?

19.

EMOTIONAL
PROGRESS

*When you're looking for ways to understand
and measure your emotional progress.*

How do we measure success in life, in the non-tangible sense? The world has wired us to understand what success means in many areas—financially, a big house, luxury cars, and a high-paying job could equal to success for some. But what about the progress we make as individuals in our personal growth journeys? Our emotional progress, our spiritual progress? How is that measured? The positive changes in our perspectives, the thoughtfulness in our responses, the greater gratitude we feel every day, the better control of our emotions…. Does this matter at all in our lives, and, if so, how much does it matter? We feel the subtle shifts happening, but we don't exactly have the language to understand this progress, because we are still searching for the words to explain what this could translate into. Do we know how to measure our journey towards becoming better versions of ourselves?

There are a few ways that I have come up with that could help a little.

1. You pause to think before you respond. One of the things I started noticing after developing a regular meditation practice was the delay in my responses when different kinds of situations came up. I wasn't quick to react anymore. When something came up, or a question was asked, often I was able to feel the space or gap right after the question —almost like it just laid there for a bit—and then I could respond. There was no rush to get the response out. It was more important for me to give a response that I could stand by, than to give a hurried response that I would have to correct later. There's a pause, there's a deep breath, and then there's the response.

2. You better understand emotions that come up. Instead of immediately identifying with your emotions that come up, you slow down and think about those emotions. You think about what they mean and do a deep-dive analysis. You also start to think about the "why." Why did you think about a situation a certain way or why did this emotional response come up?

3. You have more gratitude for day-to-day things. If you haven't been big on gratitude before, this feels like a huge shift. When you start noticing the smaller things in life that you can be grateful for, over time you realize that they all add up and actually become the big things in life. That's incredible growth in itself. This is not the kind of shift that you take lightly; it's probably not something that can happen as one huge change, but even the day-to-day observance of things working out well and feeling grateful for them can have a large impact on our lives.

4. You feel clearer about the direction you're headed in. You realize that your vision suddenly gets better than it ever has before, so life feels less blurry.

5. You delve into the past less and live in the present more. You are excited about the life you are creating. You are excited by the possibilities, the paths, the unknown. The uncertainty of life does not scare you as much anymore, because you now have more faith than fear.

6. You are happier simply because you've made that choice to be happy. Instead of doing things to make you feel happy, you start from a mentality of feeling happy and do everything from this deep-rooted place. It takes a lot of inner work to get there, but it's worth every bit of it.

7. You are more comfortable with the questions of life and don't crave answers. I often think that most of life's beauty lies in its questions and not the answers. So often we chase answers and certainty, not realizing that it is in the questions that the beautiful chaos of life unfolds. And that's actually the best part; finding the answers is just a bonus.

8. You learn to let go of what's not meant for you. When you understand that certain things and people are only meant to be in your life for a certain amount of time and to serve a certain purpose, that's immense growth—knowing that you are not tied down to anything or anyone that is not serving you anymore.

9. You have more patience. In life, I have realized that many of the problems we make up in our minds only last until we give them importance. Most times, if we are patient enough to let things ride themselves out, it will all eventually be okay. Learning to feel the emotions but letting them go, learning to let the noise fade out on its own, learning to let the clutter dissipate on its own—that's growth.

10. You are more self-aware. You know what makes you tick, and what you want from life, from yourself. You know who you want to be, what your boundaries are, how much you are willing to let people into your circle, and how many. You know when to settle and when not to. You live life more with the emotions that make you come alive and keep gravitating toward those experiences.

11. You care less about what others think and more about how you feel. This is probably the first measure or indicator of growth. When you start living a life more in alignment with your values and your feelings, you are making progress. There is nothing truer or more authentic in life than when you place your feelings over appearances.

12. You know you can ride the wave out. You've been strong enough, for long enough to know that you can ride out whatever wave life puts in front of you, and you'll be okay. You have more inner strength than you have ever felt before.

13. You know your triggers and can avoid them. You can identify your triggers, you are able to control your response to them, and you can navigate or maneuver through them.

14. You want to give love to others, simply because. When you have developed enough self-love by focusing on your life and creating one you love, you simply can't help but want to spread that to others.

15. You are more comfortable being you, whether others like it or not. Their opinion does not matter as much anymore; you now have the validation you've most needed—your own.

20.

YOU ARE ALLOWED TO TURN YOUR LIFE AROUND AT ANY TIME

*When you feel like you need to be bolder in life
than you've been—asking for what you deserve
and what you need—but you have not been
able to find the right words or voice for it.*

We often use big events in our lives like weddings, New Year's, and birthdays for a time of deep reflection and introspection, thinking about where we are in life. We look back on our accomplishments, our missteps, and where we'd like to course correct. We think about the goals we had for ourselves, and even about the person who made those goals.

We often take stock of different aspects of our lives—our health, finances, relationships, and self. For some goals it looks like we are on track to arrive where we want to be in the future, while in other cases we may be behind. We recognize the person who made some of these goals, but some others make us want to cringe. While it's great to use these pivotal times to look back and make amends to our ways, I want you to know you that you don't always have to wait for a big event to come along to make a change to your current circumstances in life.

Even though our life had a certain structure, and we were following a plan that we had for our lives, if we are unhappy right now, we are allowed to introspect and understand what's feeling off. Whether it's a small feeling in our gut or a big emotional response to something, we are allowed to act on those feelings to make our lives better than they were yesterday.

We are allowed to choose differently than we have in the past, differently than we usually do. One chosen path does not mean we have to continue on that path if it makes us unhappy today. Just because things have been a certain way, does not mean they have to remain that way. We are allowed to become different people than we have been. We can't guilt ourselves into remaining who we were and following the status quo just because we are afraid of the ripple effect this could have.

Bold choices will have ripple effects—some good, some not so good. Some expected, some unexpected. But even so, we are allowed to make different choices.

We can choose who (and how much) we let into our lives, we are allowed to change how we spend our time and energy, we are allowed to choose who we want to be and when. When we feel the urge to make a change, we should act on that urge. Some things may have worked for us for a while, but when we feel like things are not working anymore, it's time to think about what needs to shift so we are able to bring about the life we wish for. Things will not all be laid out for us, and it might not be an easy path, but that does not mean we should shy away from living life to the best of our abilities.

We may have let ourselves shrink for far too long to fit into places we have long outgrown. We may have even denied ourselves of the possibilities of a whole new life and becoming a whole new person because we didn't know how far we could push our boundaries. We were unwilling to look beyond what has been. But you must give yourself the permission you need today to rise above your fears and doubt and see what's beneath the surface. To see what's possible for you.

After all, who are we to decide what's truly possible and what isn't? If what we believe to be isn't possible, what's to say that there isn't another way that we can't see right now that can make the very thing that seems impossible, possible?

21.

SAYING YES TO MORE THINGS THAT ARE GOOD FOR YOU

When you're wondering what you need to focus on in life, and what you should let go of.

This year, say yes to more of what's good for you.

Yes to more sunshine and less gloominess.

More singing and dancing, and less worrying.

More dreaming and doing.

More living and less thinking.

Yes to more thriving, and less surviving.

Yes to more things that make you come alive, and fewer that make you feel dead on the inside.

More yeses to people who feel like sunshine.

Yes to more things that energize you, and less to what drains you.

Less reminiscing and more creating new memories.

Yes to who you're meant to be, and no to what's holding you back.

Yes to the road less traveled, however scary that might seem, and no to the traditional path.

Yes to being braver, making bolder choices, and no to what feels comfortable and safe.

Yes to what helps you grow, and no to what makes you stay the same.

Yes to newer heights, and no to lower valleys.

Yes to daring to leave the shore, and no to staying in the safe harbor.

Life is too short to be scared. Too short to say yes to all the wrong things and no to all the right ones just because one of them feels safe and the other scary.

When I had my doubts on if I should move forward with the publication of this project, my editor introduced me to some lines from a beautiful poem that helped me decide to take the leap:

Because right now there is someone

Out there with

A wound in the exact shape

Of your words.

"Why Bother" by Sean Thomas Dougherty

Acknowledgments

To my husband—my best friend and partner in life. You are our rock, the foundation upon which we have built this beautiful life together. Thank you for helping me build my wings so I could fly. We've been together a long time, but some days it feels like we are just getting started. I feel like I can conquer the world with you by my side.

To my sons, you are both pieces of my heart. So much of who I am today is because of you.

To my sister, for being there when I could not. For giving more than I could ask.

To my dad, for believing that I could accomplish anything I put my mind to and for always having high goals and dreams for me.

To my mom, who brought me into this life and gave me hope when I lost my own. I wouldn't be where I am without your support.

ABOUT THE AUTHOR

Tivoli is a passionate writer, who thinks deeply about life and draws most of her inspiration from life experiences. Born and raised in Chennai, India and now living in Atlanta, USA with her husband and two kids, both countries have significantly contributed to shaping her perspectives in life. Redefining narratives, along with the belief that we all have the ability to turn our lives around is a core principle for Tivoli.

A Chartered Accountant by profession, most of Tivoli's formal education and work experience has been in the business and finance space. Aspiring to be a published writer since 2010, this book has been a labor of love put together over many years. Through her work of writing this book, she has found a lot of fulfillment and now looks forward to sharing it with the world. *Metamorphosis* is Tivoli's first book.